HAND SHADOWS

CAMEL.

Hy Bursill Invt Et Delt

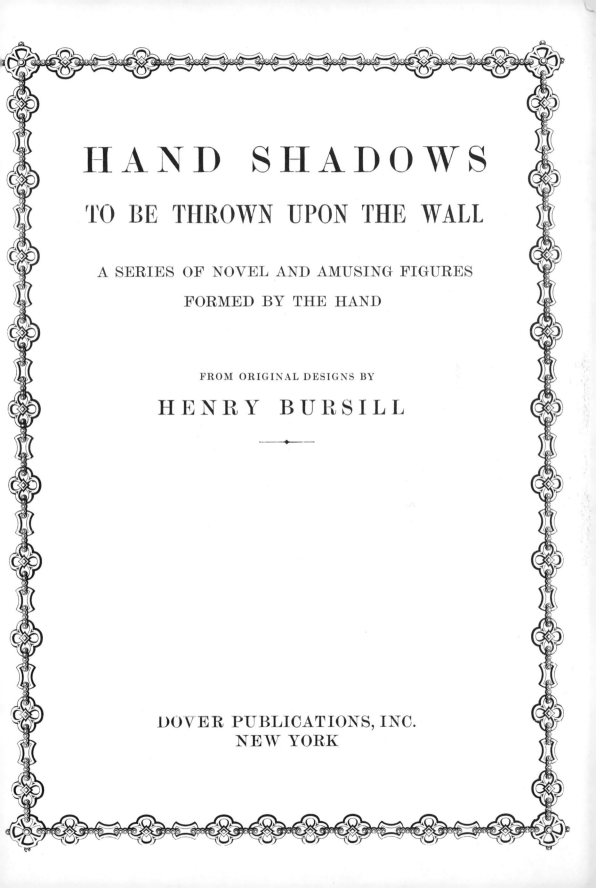

HAND SHADOWS

TO BE THROWN UPON THE WALL

A SERIES OF NOVEL AND AMUSING FIGURES

FORMED BY THE HAND

FROM ORIGINAL DESIGNS BY

HENRY BURSILL

DOVER PUBLICATIONS, INC.
NEW YORK

Published in Canada by General Publishing Company, Ltd., 30 Lesmill Road, Don Mills, Toronto, Ontario.

Published in the United Kingdom by Constable and Company, Ltd., 10 Orange Street, London WC 2.

This Dover edition, first published in 1967, is an unabridged republication of the work originally published by Griffith and Farran in 1859.

Standard Book Number: 486-21779-5

Library of Congress Catalog Card Number: 67-14250

Manufactured in the United States of America
Dover Publications, Inc.
180 Varick Street
New York, N.Y. 10014

PREFACE.

I NEED not explain how these Shadows were suggested, to any one who has seen WILKIE's picture, " The Rabbit on the Wall." But by what pains they were invented can never be revealed; for it is known to my tortured digits alone, and they, luckily for me, are dumb. I calculate that I put my ten fingers through hundreds of various exercises before my " Bird" took wing; my left little finger thrills at the memory of " Grandpapa"; and my thumbs gave in no less than twenty times before " Boy" was accomplished. Yet *now* how easy it is to make the " Duck" to quack, the " Donkey" to bray, "Toby" to wag his tail, and the " Rabbit" to munch his unsubstantial meal.

Of course the Shadows are not to be reproduced perfectly, on " one trial only"; but I believe that in each case I have drawn the due position of the fingers with such care, that the most difficult subject may be accomplished after a few minutes; nor need ingenious youth or parental fondness confine their endeavours to the sketches contained in this book. With a little ingenuity and some patience, new shadows may be produced; and not un-frequently figures appear that one never dreamed of attempting.

Other Books of Shadows have been published; but it will be seen at a glance that mine bears affinity to none. Some of my sketches were made years ago, others when a student at the Academy. Indeed, the Shadows have often been displayed on the walls of my studio, much to the amusement of fellow-students, who would, I am sure, at any time bear witness to their originality.

HENRY BURSILL

December, 1858.

HAND SHADOWS

HENRY BY BURSILL.

GRIFFITH & FARRAN,
CORNER OF ST PAUL'S CHURCH YARD

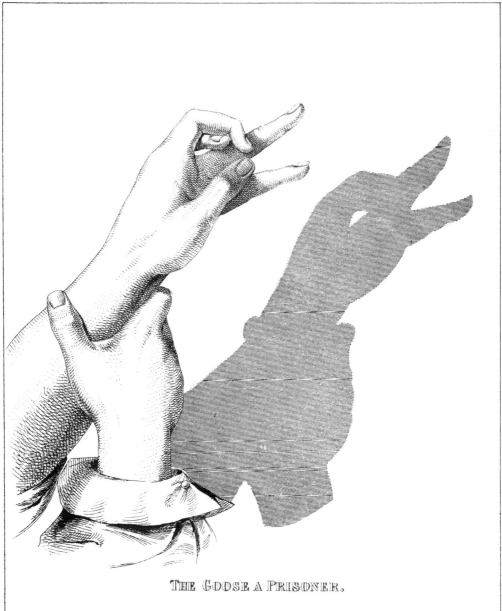

THE GOOSE A PRISONER.

H.ʸ Burvill Inᵗ Et Delᵗ

1.

DEER.

Hy Burvill Invt Et Delt

GRANDPAPA.

Hy Burvill Invt Et Delt

BUNNY.

H. Burvill Invt Et Delt.

4.

A BIRD IN FLIGHT.

Hy Burvill Invt Et Delt

GOAT.

Hy Burdill Invt Et Delt

6.

DOG TOBY.

Hy Barwell Invt Et Delt

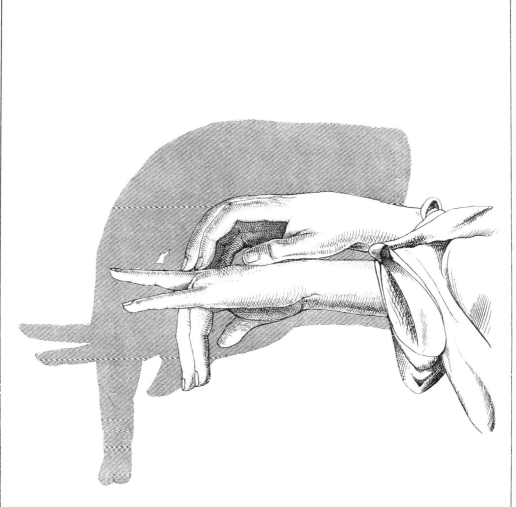

An Elephant.

8

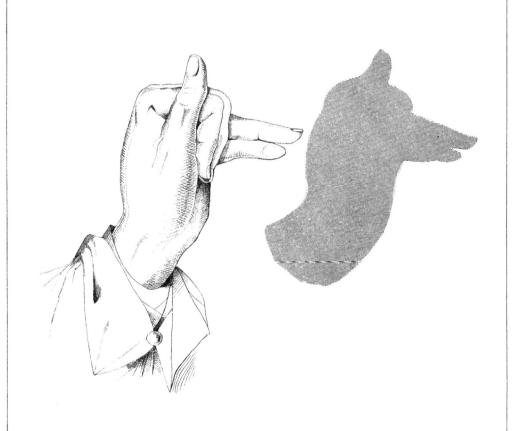

GREYHOUND.

9.

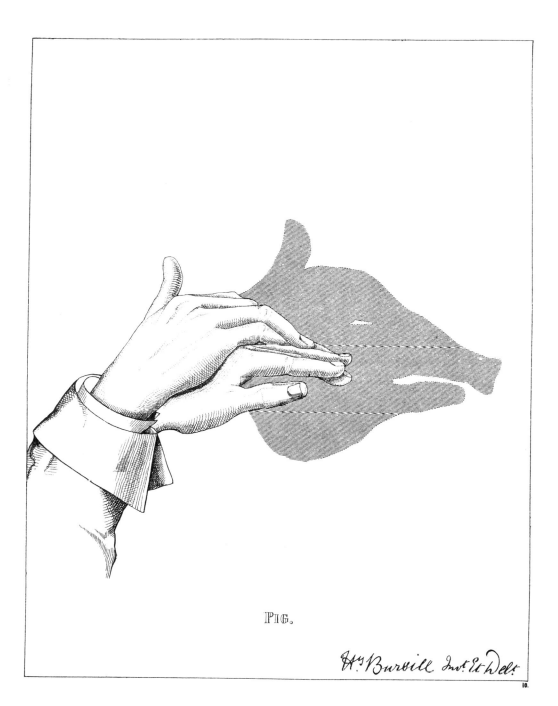

PIG.

10.

BRUIN.

H.ʸ Burvill Inᵗ Etᶜ Delᵗ

II.

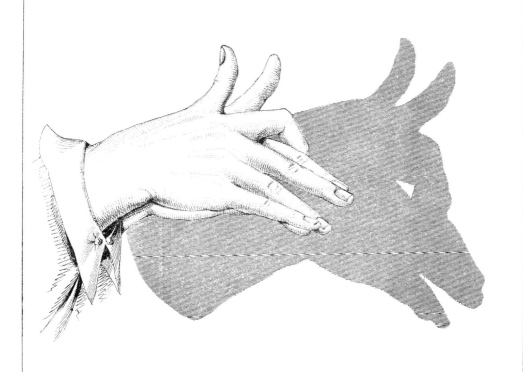

A PORTRAIT.

OLD GROWLER.

Hy Burvill Invt Et Delt

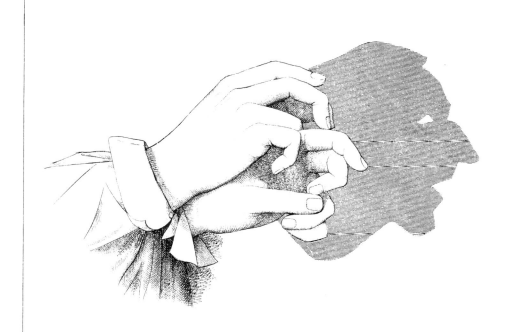

FRIGHT.

A TORTOISE.

Jn.s Barweill Inst. St.Delt.

15.

BOY.

Hy Bursill Invt Et Delt

16.

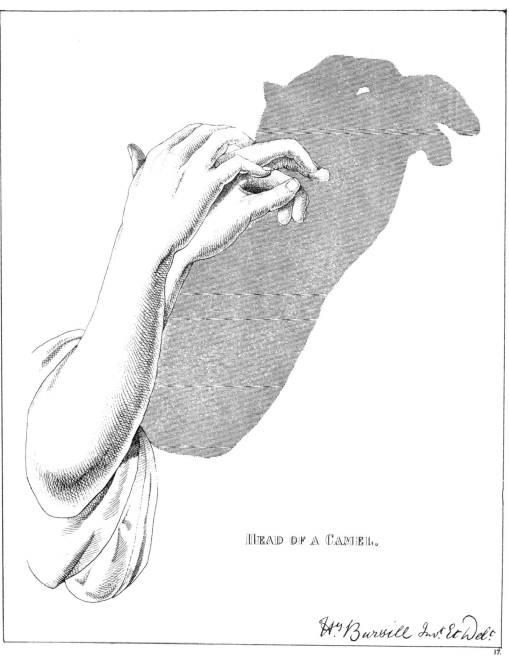

HEAD OF A CAMEL.

H.ᵞ Burvill Inᵗ. Et Delᵗ

17.